5 Butterflies

CAROL PASTERNAK

Fitzhenry & Whiteside

Published in Canada by Fitzhenry & Whiteside
195 Allstate Parkway, Markham, ON   L3R 4T8

Published in the United States by Fitzhenry & Whiteside
311 Washington Street, Brighton, MA   02135

Fitzhenry & Whiteside acknowledges with thanks the Canada Council for the Arts
and the Ontario Arts Council for their support of our publishing program.
We acknowledge the financial support of the Government of Canada through
the Canada Book Fund (CBF) for our publishing activities.

Cover and interior design by Tanya Montini
Printed in Hong Kong, China by Sheck Wah Tong Printing

Library and Archives Canada Cataloguing in Publication
Title: 5 butterflies / Carol Pasternak.
Other titles: Five butterflies
Names: Pasternak, Carol, 1954- author.
Description: Includes index.
Identifiers: Canadiana 20210259698 | ISBN 9781554554331 (hardcover)
Subjects: LCSH: Butterflies—Juvenile literature.
Classification: LCC QL544.2 .P37 2021 | DDC j595.78/9—dc23

Publisher Cataloging-in-Publication Data (U.S.)
Names: Pasternak, Carol, 1954-, author.
Title: 5 Butterflies / Carol Pasternak.
Description: Markham, Ontario : Fitzhenry & Whiteside, 2021.| Summary:
"Understand why butterflies are so important to our very existence. Learn about
the challenges caterpillars and butterflies face. Examine the wondrous day to day
changes in a caterpillar's life. Discover how you can help butterflies right in your
neighborhood" -- Provided by publisher.
Identifiers: ISBN 978-1-55455-433 -1 (hardcover)
Subjects: LCSH Butterflies —Juvenile literature. | Moths – Juvenile literature. |
Butterflies – Life cycles – Juvenile literature. | Butterfly gardening– Juvenile literature. |
BISAC: JUVENILE NONFICTION / Animals / Butterflies, Moths & Caterpillars.
Classification: LCC QL544.2P378 |DDC 599.78 – dc23

Fitzhenry & Whiteside

CONTENTS

There are about 17,500 species of butterflies in the world.

Introduction

AN INVITATION

If you ask your parents or grandparents whether they remember butterflies as they were growing up, most of them will readily tell you stories of lazy summer days spent climbing trees, picnicking in meadows, watching tadpoles in the pond turn into frogs, or enjoying an amazing assortment of butterflies dancing in the sky. Sometimes, they might say, they put a caterpillar and some leaves into a jar to watch it magically transform into something completely different!

In just one generation, however, many of those accessible open spaces have been bulldozed for factories, roads, and houses. Fields of crops have been doused with pesticides, wiping out the plants and insects that shared their space. And children and youth may enjoy less unsupervised time to just wander and wonder in nature.

Biophilia, the love of nature and living things, is an essential part of the human condition. Hortophilia, the desire to interact with, manage, and tend nature, is also deeply instilled in us. The effects of nature's qualities on health are not only spiritual and emotional but physical and neurological. I have no doubt that they reflect deep changes in the brain's physiology, and perhaps even its structure.

- Oliver Sacks, *neurologist, naturalist, historian, and author*

Nature can make you feel a part
of something bigger than yourself.

I invite you to get out and explore the natural world—the place you call home—that provides us with food, air, and water. The world of nature is not found only on documentary TV channels. You can discover it right in your neighbourhood. Plants, mammals, insects, birds, and soil connect us in ways that science is just beginning to understand. When we commune with nature, we feel a part of something much bigger than ourselves. Our sense of awe translates into well-being, physically, emotionally, and spiritually. The more you connect to it, the better you feel. The more you love it, the more you will want to protect it. And that is the only way we humans can save our world. The good news is, there is still time to act. And you will love every minute of it.

There are many paths to nature, and **Lepidoptera** (butterflies and moths) is one of them. I wrote *5 Butterflies* to ignite your curiosity about wildlife through the observation and raising of caterpillars. Your search for them will take you out of the house, to a miniature world that will astound you. So, grab your magnifying glass and let's get started!

Beautiful wood nymph caterpillar.

A few hours before it emerges, we can see the caterpillar's tiny head as it prepares to chew itself out of its ridged eggshell. The egg is attached to a milkweed leaf.

This Baltimore checkerspot, like many butterflies, is very colourful.

Is It a Butterfly or a Moth?

Before we begin our adventures, it will be helpful to learn some anatomy. All insects have a head, thorax, and abdomen. They have three pairs of legs on the thorax. Caterpillars also have **prolegs** for grip and to propel themselves. Unlike true legs, prolegs have no joints. Caterpillars breathe through openings in their sides, called spiracles. Adult butterflies and moths smell and navigate with their antennae.

While some insects have three stages in their life cycle (egg, nymph, and adult), butterflies and moths have four. They undergo complete **metamorphosis**, meaning that the first stage and the fourth stage take very different forms, often live in different habitats, and exhibit strikingly different behaviour. The four stages are egg, caterpillar (**larva**), **pupa**, and **adult** (butterfly or moth). It is important to note that all four stages are called by their species name. For example, a swallowtail egg, caterpillar, and adult are all referred to as a swallowtail. Or, if you have two eggs, three caterpillars, and

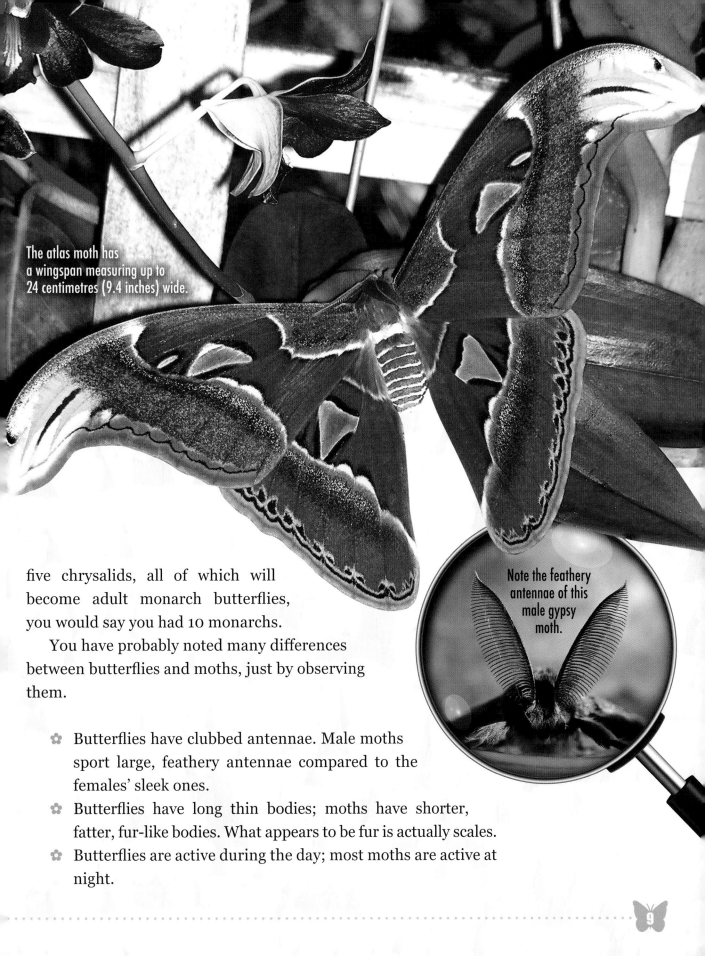

The atlas moth has a wingspan measuring up to 24 centimetres (9.4 inches) wide.

Note the feathery antennae of this male gypsy moth.

five chrysalids, all of which will become adult monarch butterflies, you would say you had 10 monarchs.

You have probably noted many differences between butterflies and moths, just by observing them.

- ❀ Butterflies have clubbed antennae. Male moths sport large, feathery antennae compared to the females' sleek ones.
- ❀ Butterflies have long thin bodies; moths have shorter, fatter, fur-like bodies. What appears to be fur is actually scales.
- ❀ Butterflies are active during the day; most moths are active at night.

✿ Butterflies are usually bigger than moths, but the largest moth, the atlas, is bigger than the largest butterfly, the birdwing.

✿ Butterflies rest with their wings closed. Most moths rest with their wings open. Some moths fold their wings on their back.

✿ Butterflies are usually more brightly coloured than moths, but the moth exceptions can be extremely vibrant.

✿ A butterfly pupa is called a chrysalis. Moths often spin a silk cocoon to protect the pupa. Sometimes, they crawl into the soil to make their pupa.

Dogbane tiger moth resting with its wings folded on its back.

Butterflies have clubbed antennae, like this red admiral.

This giant swallowtail's abdomen is long and less fur-like than a moth abdomen.

Anatomy of a Moth and Butterfly

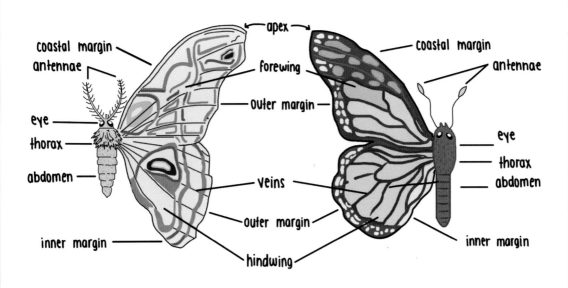

apex

coastal margin

antennae

eye

thorax

abdomen

forewing

Outer margin

veins

Outer margin

hindwing

inner margin

coastal margin

antennae

eye

thorax

abdomen

inner margin

Most moths look rather drab and have fat, fur-like bodies, like this tussock moth.

This monarch is resting on native cup plant. You can tell it's a male from the black spot on each of the two hind wings.

Miraculous Monarch

The monarch *Danaus plexippus* is North America's most treasured butterfly. It glides gracefully through meadows and yards, displaying large, boldly decorated orange wings. Yet, it is not its beauty or size that place it above all others—it is its incredible story.

From the time it hatches from its pinhead-sized egg, its life is a series of one miracle after another.

Female monarchs lay about 400 eggs on their one and only host plant, milkweed. Only about four eggs will survive the challenges ahead to become an adult. In three to five days, depending on the temperature, the caterpillar will chew its way out of its egg case, then turn around to devour it. The egg case contains the necessary protein for the monarch's first meal.

There are 127 species of milkweed and each has evolved to protect itself from being eaten. Most, like common milkweed, have fine hairs the hatchling must shave off before it can chomp into the leaf. The leaf contains milky white latex, which can gush out and

A monarch butterfly lays its eggs
only on milkweed plants

A monarch egg rests on
a milkweed flower bud.

A newly emerged caterpillar
eating its egg case.

choke the newly emerged caterpillar, or glue its jaws shut. To avoid this fate, the caterpillar nibbles a shallow circular trench around a dime-sized portion of the leaf to slow down that flow of sap before taking its first real bite. Still, the plant wins the battle one-third of the time and the caterpillar dies.

If all goes well, the monarch caterpillar will grow rapidly, devouring milkweed day and night for less than two weeks. It will **moult**, or shed its skin, five times, before becoming a chrysalis. More often than not, it will wander from its milkweed, up to 10 metres (32 feet), in search of a safe and protected hiding place. It could be a sturdy leaf, a twig in a shrub, or even the underside of a wood fence or a roof overhang. The caterpillar will tirelessly crisscross its head back and forth over an area of a few inches, weaving silk from a gland under its mouth, called a **spinneret**.

Milkweed sap, also called latex, can be fatal to a caterpillar.

This monarch is chewing a trench. Do you see how it has shaved off the fine hairs on the milkweed?

If you discover a chewed milkweed bud, look for a monarch nearby. This one has just moulted. Soon, its old face will fall off.

All animals can be identified according to the International Code for Zoological Nomenclature. Regardless of the languages used around the world, these standard scientific names, derived from Latin or Greek, are universally understood. Using these names helps avoid confusion. For example:

❀ **Monarch** *Danaus plexippus*
❀ **American lady** *Vanessa virginiensis*
❀ **Black swallowtail** *Papilio polyxenes*
❀ **Question mark** *Polygonia interrogationis*
❀ **Cecropia** *Hyalophora cecropia*

Gradually, it will focus on a spot the size of a lentil, until a silk "button" is formed. The caterpillar attaches itself to this button with its rear claspers, in order to hang in a "J" shape for about 16 hours. During that time, most of its caterpillar organs dissolve while its butterfly features begin to grow. Soon after its filaments twist and its body straightens the skin on its head will split open! The start of its chrysalis will burst out as its final skin shrivels upward. Then, seemingly out of nowhere, the short, black toothpick-like **cremaster** will pop out and "search" for the silk button. When it touches it, the new chrysalis will whirl vigorously to embed the tiny Velcro-like hooks on the cremaster into the silk button. We call these gyrations its **pupa dance**.

When it is secure, the monarch will perfect the chrysalis, decorating it with gold dots. One evening, about two weeks later, the orange and black wings become visible through the transparent **cuticle**. The monarch will emerge the next morning. It will pump the fluid from its pudgy abdomen into its wings, which will become full sized in less than half an hour. It will hang for several hours, slowly opening and closing its wings until they are dry. It may fly to a better place to spend the rest of the day quietly maturing. The next day, it will begin its mission of eating, mating, and laying eggs, for about a month. That is, unless it emerges in mid-August or later, in which case it will live as long as 9 months. How is that possible? Unable to withstand a freezing winter, it will migrate to a place where it won't spend energy on reproducing and will live in a state of semi-hibernation.

Most monarchs living to the west of the North American Rockies overwinter in California. A small number of them migrate to Mexico. They gather along the west coast for about four months. During the winter of 2020/2021, this population plummeted to fewer than 2,000, a decline of 99.9 percent since the 1980s. Destruction, degradation and neglect of overwintering sites, climate change, and overuse of insecticides are all contributing factors.

Every day is a struggle to survive for a monarch. Predators flock to the milkweed patch looking for a nourishing monarch meal. Eggs are enjoyed by some species of earwigs, spiders, ants, and mites.

This chrysalis is secure. It will not fall off even in severe weather.

The period between moults is called an instar. When a caterpillar hatches, it is in its first instar.

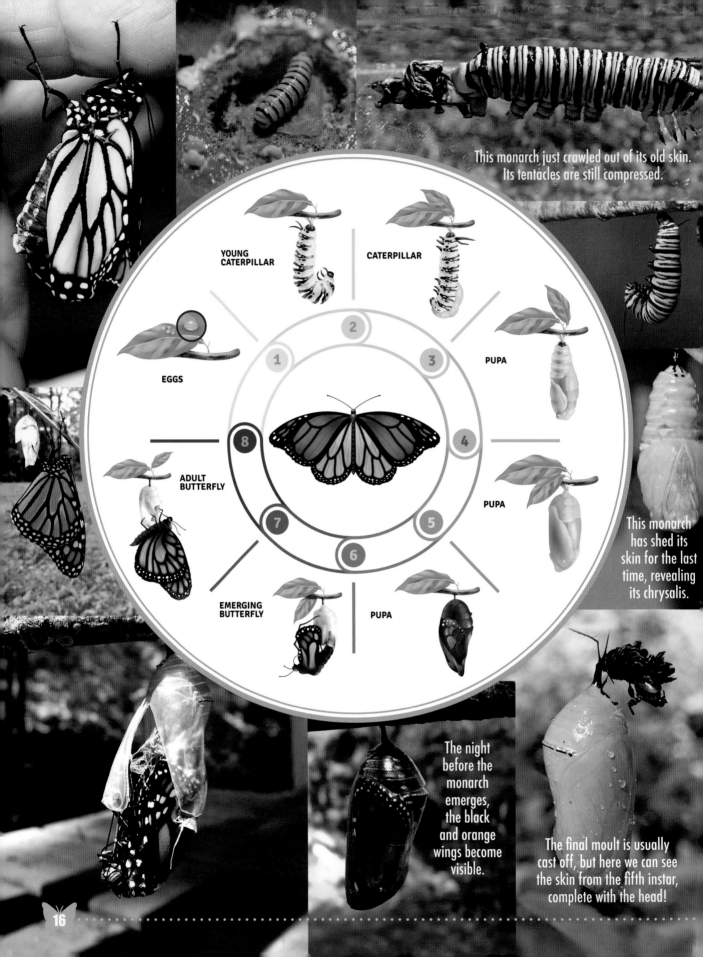

This monarch just crawled out of its old skin. Its tentacles are still compressed.

YOUNG CATERPILLAR

CATERPILLAR

EGGS

1

2

3

PUPA

8

ADULT BUTTERFLY

4

7

5

6

PUPA

EMERGING BUTTERFLY

PUPA

This monarch has shed its skin for the last time, revealing its chrysalis.

The night before the monarch emerges, the black and orange wings become visible.

The final moult is usually cast off, but here we can see the skin from the fifth instar, complete with the head!

The bitter, somewhat toxic sap the caterpillar ingests from the milkweed can deter some predators, but stink bugs, wasps, assassin bugs, small milkweed bugs, spiders, frogs, and lizards don't seem to mind it. Dragonflies and praying mantids feast on the adults.

Diseases and **parasites** can attack the caterpillars at every stage. A parasite is a living **organism** that depends on another organism for food or shelter. The tachinid fly is an example of a parasite that kills its host. The dreaded fly lays its eggs on defenceless caterpillars and, upon hatching, the fly larva burrows its way in and proceeds to eat all of the caterpillar's nonessential organs. Depending on which instar is invaded, the monarch might still be able to form its chrysalis. When the fly larva is ready to pupate, it will parachute out of the chrysalis, sliding down a white mucous "string," making its pupa after it lands. By that time, the monarch is dead, and the chrysalis has turned brown.

The dreaded tachinid fly.

Can you see where the fly larva exited the chrysalis?

LOCATION MAP OF MONARCH SPECIES

Protecting Monarchs

You can protect monarch butterflies (and other caterpillars) from predators by raising them indoors. This allows you to witness firsthand the changes the monarch goes through to grow to *2,000 times its birth weight* in two weeks. Although I have been raising monarchs for 40 years, watching these miraculous developments never fails to amaze me. Most people can't wait to check the rearing containers several times a day, and even take them to school or work so as not to miss a thing. They share the butterflies' abrupt changes in development with more and more people, answering their questions as they observe, learn, and pass along their newfound knowledge.

If you decide to raise monarchs (the best summer hobby EVER), you can observe the mesmerizing process of moulting. With silk from its spinneret, the caterpillar lays down a mat to secure itself to its milkweed leaf. It remains still for about 24 hours while it makes changes inside. Then it takes in air, to separate itself from the old skin, and its head starts to fall off. It crawls out of the old skin, which

This recently moulted caterpillar's face is about to fall off!

Place your leaves eggs-side up in a reusable or take-out container.

gathers behind it. Eventually, it casts off the old face cap and promptly grows a new one! Then it turns around to eat the old skin.

The process of raising butterflies is not as difficult as you might think. All you need to do is plant or find milkweed, then search for eggs and caterpillars. Eggs will most often be found on the underside of leaves, but you should check the buds, flowers, stem, and even the pods. Cut off the entire section that the monarchs are on and place it in a plastic takeout or salad container. It just needs to be tall enough for the emerging monarch to hang from the empty case, about 20 centimetres (8 inches). Young specimens do not need holes in the top; in fact, they will escape through them. Open the container every day to check for mould and remove any that you find. This will also provide fresh air. Wipe off any condensation. As the monarchs grow, punch a few holes in the top, add fresh leaves, and remove old leaves and poop, called **frass**. I like to use a small pet container for my larger caterpillars.

Wash the container daily. Start with just two or three eggs or caterpillars, until you get the hang of it. They eat a lot more than you'd think. Add an extra leaf before you go to bed; they eat all night.

Using the information on this tag, the finder can report the butterfly to Monarch Watch, who can trace its starting point.

Soon, you will see the life you have nurtured pop out of its chrysalis as a completely different being. It may just take your breath away. An hour after it emerges, it will easily crawl onto your finger, where you can examine every detail. The monarch will be best able to defend itself the day after it emerges, but most people release it when it starts flapping around, at about four hours old. Just take the rearing container outside and open it. Imagine how you will feel when you see it taking its first flight into freedom.

Would you believe there are thousands of people, on standby, ready to help you with any question you might have when raising your first monarchs? It's true! You can get almost instant answers to your queries from the Facebook group The Beautiful Monarch. Welcome to the club!

It is not necessary to go on a mission to rescue every monarch you find. Its predators need to live, too. An ecosystem thrives when all members are present in perfect balance. And why deprive other people of the thrill of discovering caterpillars? I love to go searching for butterflies with friends. We feed off each other's delight with each discovery of an egg or a caterpillar. And while we are in the meadow or ravine, we inevitably uncover interesting mystery creatures that require further investigation. Insects are everywhere, working hard to survive. Fungi pop out from the ground and trees, chirps need to be investigated, logs turned over, and ponds and creeks explored. Bring your camera or your sketch pad!

For many years, I attended an adult summer camp in Haliburton, Ontario. Of course, I had to bring all my caterpillars and chrysalises with me. I displayed them on a banquet table at the back of the mess hall, along with life cycle information. Campers could regularly be seen staring with awe into the rearing containers, reporting to me when they witnessed a moult—even calling to others as a monarch started to make its chrysalis. A crowd gathered each time someone shouted, "pupa dance!"

Every day after lunch, I held my greatly anticipated release ceremony attended by about 30 people. I described a different aspect of the monarch's life each time. For example, monarchs born in May, June, and the

These are some of the countless treasures you can find in natural areas, if you slow down to look.

Tree frog.

Camouflaged Cicada.

I found this successful spider at Presqu'ile Provincial Park, ON, during the park's annual monarch tagging event.

first half of August in Canada live for about a month. Those born later, in August or September, live up to nine months. Amazing! Then I explained how the tiny sticker I was about to place on the monarch's wing, with its unique letters and numbers, would help scientists track the path of the migration.

One day, I had four monarchs to release. Each time, I gave this honour to a different camper. In accordance with our understanding of a Native American legend, we symbolically whispered a wish to the monarch, hoping it would take it to the gods for us. Then we watched each butterfly take its first flight. Usually, it would fly high and around us, choosing a nearby tree to get its bearings before starting to fly south. The third monarch was not so lucky. To our shock and horror, a blue jay swooped by, snagged it in its beak, and paraded it in front of us. After we recovered, we tagged and released the final monarch. The following February, I learned from Monarch Watch that it had been found by a guide at one of the monarch sanctuaries in Mexico, after a journey of 4,000 kilometres (2,500 miles)! Wow!

It is not easy for a monarch to travel alone to a place it has never been. Along the journey, it could be attacked by dragonflies, lizards,

As part of the circle of life in the monarch sanctuaries, orioles, grosbeaks and mice dine on monarch abdomens.

frogs, and praying mantises, or caught by spiders. It could be sprayed with insecticide or hit by a car; it might not find enough **nectar plants** to sustain it; or it might succumb to a blizzard or a tornado. If it makes it to the overwintering grounds in Mexico and doesn't get eaten by birds or mice during its four-month stay, and then back to Texas or other Gulf coast states, it will surely be thin and tattered. Still, in an impressive feat of endurance, it will lay its eggs on the newly erupted milkweed. By the time those eggs become butterflies, the milkweed they ate as caterpillars, will be old. The new monarchs will fly even farther north in search of fresh sprouts. That generation will reach the northern United States or Canada. It is the later-season monarchs that forego mating and head to Mexico. In all, it takes four or five generations of monarchs to complete the round trip.

Monarchs need the specialized climate they find high in a small area of mountains 100 kilometres (62 miles) northwest of Mexico City. There, the canopy of fir trees holds the right amount of moisture, and the temperature is ideal for a semi-hibernating butterfly. The tree trunks radiate heat, and the canopy holds it in, providing some protection from occasional freezes.

A spectacular show for visitors, the weight of the monarchs, each weighing less than a gram, bends the branches of the oyamel trees.

The land these monarchs roost on has always belonged to Indigenous people of Mexico, managed either privately or by communities. These people made their living by farming and logging. In 1975, Dr. Fred Urquhart and his wife, Norah, "discovered" that the monarchs in those lands originated in Canada and the United States. As a young boy, Fred had reclined among the wildflowers at Scarborough Bluffs in Toronto, Ontario, wondering where his favourite butterfly went for the winter. He went on to spend 40 years on his obsession to find the monarchs' overwintering grounds.

Nature lovers lobbied the Mexican government to protect the Oyamel Forest. In 1986, the government ordered that 16,000 hectares (40,000 acres) be reserved as monarch habitat and for monitoring. In 2000, the protected area was enlarged, with core and buffer zones, and named the Monarch Butterfly Biosphere Reserve. In the same year, various government organizations and the World Wildlife Fund came together to create Fondo Monarca. This endowment fund was started with contributions from private donors and government. Payments from the interest on this money are distributed to property owners who continue to conserve monarch habitat. In 2008, **UNESCO** (United Nations Educational, Scientific, and Cultural Organization) designated the Monarch Butterfly Biosphere Reserve as a Natural World Heritage Site.

Even with the support of Fondo Monarca, poverty in the biosphere drives people to cut down trees. They need firewood for their stoves and the income from logs to feed their families. The monarchs' winter home is also threatened by illegal logging by organized crime in and near the monarch sanctuaries.

What can be done to save the forests? Forest rangers deter some illegal loggers, but it is risky work to confront organized crime, and neither Fondo Monarca nor the Mexican government provides adequate money for forest rangers. Several organizations offer conservation education to landowners living near the monarch sanctuaries. **Forests for Monarchs** has planted 9 million trees since 1997. The **Monarch Butterfly Fund** supports reforestation projects in the Reserve, and workshops to local communities on how to build fuel-efficient stoves, water cisterns, and latrines. **Monarchs Across Georgia** sends a teacher to schools near the sanctuaries to teach the importance of the overwintering grounds and conservation.

Ecotourism now provides jobs so that the Indigenous people who previously relied

Wood stove used by a food vendor in a Mexican butterfly sanctuary.

Reserva de la Biosfera
Mariposa Monarca
Reglamento
Estás entrando a la zona de observación de la colonia de mariposa monarca.
Atiende las indicaciones y recomendaciones de los guías locales.

Tourists are welcomed, fed, entertained, cared for, and educated to leave no trace behind them. Of the four sanctuaries open to the public, El Rosario boasts the greatest number of butterflies.

ABOVE: This was the first effort by students ages six to 12. I later learned that most of them had never held a paint brush.

TOP: In only a few months, the students' artwork blossomed.

on logging and farming can make their living from the forests. Guides provide horses to take tourists up the mountains and keep them at a safe distance from the butterflies. Vendors provide food and souvenirs, while nearby towns offer accommodation.

Prior to my first trip to the sanctuaries in 2016, I thought about what I could do to help save the forests. I learned that tourists complained there were not enough souvenirs, and the locals complained there was no work. I also discovered that school children did not have art classes, because there was no budget for art supplies.

I went to my local craft shop in Toronto, asked for advice from the staff, and loaded up on paints and brushes. I saved plastic egg cartons and container lids to use as pallets and cut out and copied photos of monarchs. I packed it all in a suitcase I scavenged from someone's

garbage and took it to the school in a small town beside a sanctuary. In less than 30 minutes, in my broken Spanish, I taught 60 primary students in a small town next to a **monarch sanctuary** how to paint monarch butterflies on small rocks to sell to tourists. I did not pick up a brush myself, as I do not have the talent to paint monarchs. Several months later, the teacher reported that the children became excited about school, skipped less, got along with everyone better, learned from each other, and started to express themselves through art. Their work grew more and more detailed, interesting, and attractive.

Most of the money earned is allotted to school outings and supplies, while some goes directly to the student artists. For the first time, the principal rented a bus and took the children to the museum in Mexico City. They also participate proudly in local exhibitions where they teach and learn from other artists. They have expanded their selection to Christmas tree ornaments, bags, and purses, and are proud to sell them to visitors. They have learned business skills that will serve them well in life.

ABOVE: Students and teachers pack up their work, to be sent to the US to fulfill online orders.

TOP: The students were so proud to take home 50 pesos, or about three dollars.

With a little research, and the help of the owner, I chose a selection of native plants from a native plant nursery to add to my back yard.

Inviting Butterflies to your Garden

From now on, I'd like you to consider your yard, school, library, community centre, fire station, and just about everywhere else, as **habitat**. The development of houses, roads, workplaces, and farms destroys about 2,400 hectares (6,000 acres) of wildlife habitat in the United States daily. That's equivalent to 4,500 football fields *each and every day*! We need to make the best use of the natural areas we still have and make efforts to prevent further development where possible. In Canada, less than 5 per cent of Prince Edward Island, New Brunswick, and **ecozones** in southern Ontario and Quebec is government protected. Some scientists have estimated that up to 40% of insect species in North America might be at risk for extinction in coming decades. The main causes are loss of habitat, use of pesticides, and climate change.

The total surface of lawns in the United States has been estimated, with the help of satellite technology, to be somewhere between the

size of New York State and that of Texas. When you think about it, grass is pretty boring. It is also harmful. We drown it in fertilizer and chemicals to kill the grubs, and when it rains, all that washes into our lakes and rivers to kill the wildlife there. The chemicals we pour on our lawns are causing cancer, allergies, and other ailments in our children, pets, golfers, landscapers, and others who work and play around grass, according to the Natural Resources Defence Council (NRCD.org). The US Environmental Protection Agency reports that each gas-powered lawn mower produces as much air pollution as 43 new automobiles driven 19,000 kilometres (12,000 miles) per year, while lawn care produces six billion kilograms (13 billion pounds) of toxic pollutants per year. And up to half of our drinking water is used to water the lawn, about 34 billion litres (9 billion gallons) of water per day in the United States.

It's time to replace the greater part of lawns with **native plants**. Native plants are those that were in North America before the arrival of European settlers, about 400 years ago. Until then, insects, plants, and other wildlife co-existed in balance by adapting to each other's presence. Europeans brought their plants with them, along with any insect eggs hiding in the soil. The native insects rarely ate these new plants, and there were few, if any, predators eating the new insects. It

My neighbours love my new front garden, and I love to talk with them about it.

can take thousands, or even millions, of years for ecosystems to adjust to foreign **flora** and **fauna**. All plants introduced by settlers are non-native, also known as alien, exotic, and ornamental. Some of these plants have naturalized, meaning they will reproduce without our help.

Native plants, on the other hand, have evolved with the insects. The existing insects learned to eat the native plants and, in turn, developed systems to slow the damage from consuming these plants or to rebound after it. Along with the vast assortment of predators, native plants keep the ecosystem thriving in perfect balance.

More than 5,000 non-native plants are invasive! That means they spread quickly and are strong enough to kill, or crowd out, the native plants around them. In southern Ontario, where I live, invasive dog-strangling vine has taken over our ravines. Where just 10 years ago, the thriving monarch butterfly population took advantage of vast expanses of common milkweed, I see mostly vines. This vine crawls up saplings and takes them down; the vines' strong roots extend to prevent native plants from spreading theirs. They have now made their way into private

Very few insects or native plants live in this patch of invasive garlic mustard.

Last year's invasive dog strangling vine crawled right up the trees! And it has killed all the milkweed that was in this spot just a few years ago.

The purple flowering thin-stemmed vine has engulfed this milkweed. Strangled above the ground, with roots crowded out below, this milkweed will not live long.

gardens, slowly destroying them before the homeowners notice what is happening. It can take years of digging to be rid of them, a project much too daunting for large areas.

When you see thickets of any particular plant or vine, it is called a **monoculture**. Across the United States and Canada, you'll find monocultures of one or more of Japanese knotweed, garlic mustard, phragmites, oriental bittersweet, autumn and Russian olive, Bradford pear, butterfly bush (yes, the one everyone loves because adult butterflies flock to it), and mile-a-minute. The story becomes worse when we factor in the diseases and destructive bugs, like Chestnut blight and Japanese beetles, that come along with the new ornamentals we continue to import.

We continue to **propagate** alien plants because we like them. A good example is periwinkle, a creeping groundcover that produces attractive purple flowers. Landscapers recommend it, as it

grows well in the shady areas of your yard. Our insects cannot digest this foreign plant. Unimpeded, it winds up in the wild, crowding out the native plants on which the butterflies and moths lay their eggs. With fewer host plants in the meadows and woodlots, there are fewer caterpillars for the birds to feed to their young, and fewer insects for the hedgehogs, bats, armadillos, shrews, and thousands of other species of **insectivores** and **omnivores**. We are literally starving wildlife.

You can start your butterfly garden with the smallest selection of **host plants**, which caterpillars eat, and **nectar plants**, which butterflies eat. You will need to learn which butterflies live in your region. Go to butterfliesandmoths.org and click on *Species Profiles* and choose *Regional Checklists*. You can then click on any butterfly or moth to view a photo of it, along with a list of host plants. If you live in the United States, you might find

Many birds, like this White-eyed vireo require over a thousand caterpillars to raise one brood of chicks.

Black-eyed Susans and pearly everlasting.

gardenswithwings.com more user friendly, as it shows photos of both the butterflies and the host and nectar plants. My favourite method, however, is with a book. The advantage is that the authors of the books I recommend have already chosen the most common butterflies, and it is easy to learn as much or as little as you wish to about them. Books are listed in the Resources section at the back of this book.

You're on your way! Now, where to find the native plants.

Most people who shop at big box stores or garden centres want their plants to be free of insects. That's why the stores order the plants treated with insecticides. Some insecticides are systemic, meaning that even if you cut off the existing leaves, the new ones will be toxic. You want your plants to *support* insects. If the garden centre is small, you might be able to trust the manager if she tells you that the native plants at her store have not been sprayed. Don't trust anyone but the manager; other staff might not really know. Too many people have fed poisoned leaves to their caterpillars, only to watch them vomit and die.

Your best bet is to find a native plant grower in your area. Fortunately, there are organizations that exist for the purpose of promoting safe native plants. One is the North American Native Plant Society. Visit nanps.org. The drop-down menu from *Growing Native Plants* lists *Commercial Growers* by province and state. If you don't see your region, just search online for your province or state, followed by *native plant nurseries.*

It's up to you to change the current ideal of the perfect lawn. Wild is the new beautiful!

Monarch Watch is one of many organizations to which you can apply to have your garden certified.

When your butterfly garden is certified, you create teaching moments for everyone who sees it.

American lady, upper side.

American Lady

I had been raising monarch butterflies for 30 years by the time I attended my first butterfly festival. One vendor had a small selection of native plants. As I was anxious to experience the life cycle of a different butterfly species, I asked the proprietor whether she had any host plants that might bring butterflies to my tiny garden in the suburbs. She picked up a pearly everlasting and promised me that American ladies *Vanessa virginiensis* would find the plant in my garden. I was not so sure. "My garden faces a busy main street," I told her. "They will find it," she assured me. Seeing the scepticism in my face, she added, "And if they don't, please come to my nursery and take as many caterpillars as you like. They will be eating my inventory!" I decided to invest the eight dollars for two plants and headed home, not believing for a second that I would ever spot an American lady butterfly in my yard.

I dutifully planted the fuzzy bluish green seedlings. To my surprise, they survived beneath the snow all winter, then pushed up new little

Newly hatched American lady caterpillars.

American lady laying eggs on pearly everlasting.

shoots as soon as the temperature warmed up. From my kitchen window, I see the constant traffic on the other side of my fence, and beyond that, huge apartment buildings and department stores. One May day, I leapt up screaming to my partner to run to the kitchen window. A butterfly had flown into our garden and landed on the pearly everlasting! It perched on one leaf, then another, and another.

American lady caterpillar making a nest in which to hide.

American lady chrysalis.

When it finally left, I ran out to inspect the plants. I could not find any eggs, until I inspected closely with my magnifying glass. Success!

The friendly American Lady jams its eggs under the fine hairs of pussytoes and pearly everlasting, among other plants. In the spring, when she's on a mission to lay her eggs within her two- to three-week life span, you can get close enough to this butterfly to get a really good look at the process. A few days after the eggs hatch, the young caterpillars make unattractive silk nests in order to hide from predators; many gardeners apply insecticide or destroy the dwelling by hand. They don't know that the plant will recover fully, and that, if left alone, the caterpillars will become magnificent butterflies. The caterpillars themselves are beautiful and provide food to ever-hungry baby birds.

With wings closed, the American lady is brown and pink, with white lines and brown eye spots. With wings open, it looks completely different! The butterfly is orange, brown, and black with small white spots. If you raise them, you will be fascinated to observe all the changes and details up close.

American lady, bottom side.

Scientists do not know everything about the American lady's overwintering strategy. Some hibernate, some fly south for the winter, some fly north for the summer, and some live year-round in the south. Those that migrate or hibernate, generally have three or four broods (generations) between May and November. Do you get it? Will you become the entomologist who fills in the blanks?

The largest populations of American ladies can be found in southern Canada, through the United States, as well as northern South America.

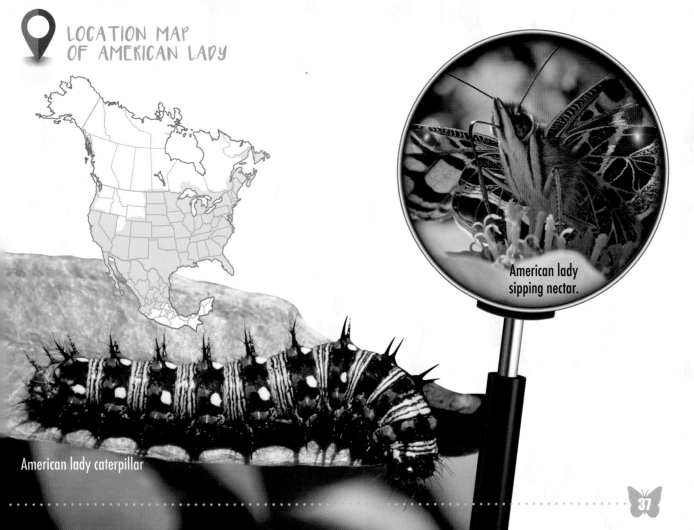

LOCATION MAP
OF AMERICAN LADY

American lady
sipping nectar.

American lady caterpillar

Many butterfly houses display so many chrysalids, you just might see a butterfly hatch!

Butterfly Farming

Butterflies are farmed all over the world. These businesses are generally small family operations that provide chrysalises to butterfly exhibits and caterpillars to schools. Most Canadian butterfly farms are located in Ontario. During the summer, they provide monarchs and painted ladies for release at special events, such as weddings and funerals. There are more than 100 butterfly ranchers, as they are sometimes called, in the United States. They raise such domestic butterflies as monarchs, zebra longwings, painted ladies, swallowtails, sulphurs, buckeyes, queens, julias, fritillaries, and red admirals, as well as moths, including lunas, cecropias, and polyphemus.

Like any livestock farming, butterfly farming is a seven-days-a-week venture. Caterpillars are ravenous and must be fed and cleaned every day, all under the most sterile conditions. A challenge for every butterfly farmer is to grow enough food for all the hungry mouths. Each species requires a different host plant, which needs to be sown and tended to on a regular basis. When the butterflies emerge, they must have access to nectar substitutes like fructose water or Gatorade, or fresh or rotting fruit, depending on the species.

The butterfly farming industry we know today was founded in Costa Rica in 1984 by Joris Brinckerhoff, a former Peace Corps volunteer and his wife, Maria Sabido. While hitchhiking, Joris had a chance encounter with a butterfly enthusiast who informed him about the butterfly exhibits that were being created in England. In the early 1970s, the first true butterfly house was established on an island in the English Channel. It was enormously successful, and, by 1986, there were more than 40 butterfly houses on the British mainland.

With no experience or education about butterflies, crushing transportation costs, laws that prohibited the export of pupae, pre-internet communication, no examples

At Cambridge Butterfly Conservatory in Ontario, you can get this close to the chrysalids.

to follow, and very little money, Joris and Maria launched Costa Rica Entomological Supply (CRES). At the time, Costa Rica was known for its far-sighted efforts in conservation. Joris and Maria saw the opportunity to provide rural people with jobs, while at the same time conserving the countryside with host plants and flowers rather than new cash crops. Thirty-five years later, sustainable butterfly farming in Costa Rica provides employment to hundreds of families. In Kenya and Tanzania, more than 700 households, many of them previously earning a meagre living from illegal logging, now protect those same forests in favour of butterfly rearing. Similar conservation success stories have been reported from the Philippines, India, and Papua New Guinea.

In 1988, butterfly houses spread from England to North America. The first one, Butterfly World, in Coconut Grove Florida, is still the

This lucky visitor got to photograph swallowtails puddling at Brenda's Butterfly Habitat in Michigan.

largest in the world. Its founder, Ron Boender, like so many other butterfly farmers, has turned his hobby into conservation advocacy. He established the Bring Back the Butterflies Campaign in 1988. The goal of this program was to educate and to supply free butterfly gardening materials specific to each region to anyone interested. Wildly successful, it has resulted in thousands of new butterfly habitats and an increase in butterfly populations across the continent.

Today, butterfly houses can be found in British Columbia, Alberta, Ontario, Quebec, Newfoundland, as well as most US states. If you are lucky enough to travel, look up local exhibits. Many of them display tropical butterflies imported from all over the world. They are housed in warm, bright, humid surroundings, with water features. The varied butterflies are dazzling. They flutter about, lighting on beautiful nectar plants, and sometimes ... on you. Usually, you can see the emerging room, where butterflies hatch from the most elaborate chrysalids. It is hard to describe the overwhelming feeling of tranquility and connection to nature that one can find in these lush, tropical oases.

Butterflies are among the few animals raised for the sole purpose of setting them free.

Another kind of butterfly house showcases butterflies native to that area. You may be allowed to feed them artificial nectar from a cotton swab! Imagine the pictures you could take. Even more exciting, is that you can go on a caterpillar hunt, because the exhibit includes host plants. You can discover the whole life cycle, from egg through caterpillar, chrysalis, and adult. You may even chance upon the butterflies mating, and **ovipositing**!

Have you ever been to an agricultural fair? Many major fairs in Canada and the United States welcome a pioneer of the butterfly farming industry, David Bohlken. His travelling exhibits have entertained and educated millions of people. If you are willing to line up, you'll understand why 80,000 people did just that in 2019 at the Minnesota State Fair, the largest agricultural fair in the world.

For Bohlken, as for most butterfly farmers, their business is as much about saving our precious butterflies as it is for making a living. In 2012, his wife, Jane Breckenridge, decided to return to her ancestral land to set up a butterfly farm. "It's a calling to protect and restore God's creatures," she says. "It's nothing short of a miracle every time I see one come out." But there was more to it than that. Breckenridge saw it as a way to provide sustainable, eco-friendly work to Oklahoma First Nations in desperate need. It was such a good idea that many organizations offered assistance, including the US Department of Fish and Wildlife and US Department of Agriculture. They provided funding to restore native meadows and to

Victoria Butterfly Gardens in British Columbia receives thousands of pupae every month. This shipment is from the Philippines.

provide workshops to train Indigenous young people in the science and business of butterfly farming. The project is called Natives for Natives. You can learn more about it at nativebutterflies.org.

Many butterfly farmers supply scientists with specimens for their research. Since 2001, Shady Oak Butterfly Farm, founded by Edith Smith, has provided tens of thousands of butterflies, at every stage of their life cycle. Studies have focused on such topics as monarch migration, what goes on inside a chrysalis, and chemicals toxic to butterflies. The research has resulted in at least one strain of genetically modified (GMO) corn being taken off the market, and a change in the way mosquito spray is applied. In 2011, farmed butterflies were used to discover that the **proboscis** functions as much like a sponge as a straw! Prior to this revelation, it was generally thought that the proboscis functioned like an elephant's trunk, to suck up water, or in the case of a butterfly, nectar.

A universal symbol of hope, change, perseverance, and spirituality, butterflies can add extra meaning to special occasions. Event hosts are encouraged to take a moment to educate the public about the value, life, and plight of butterflies. Instructions are usually included. Generally, live butterflies are shipped in **glassine** envelopes that are kept in their shipping cooler until minutes before the butterflies are to be released. They simply "sleep" when it is cool, much like the monarchs do during the winter in the cool mountains of Mexico.

This cooled monarch will sleep comfortably until its release.

Some people feel it is cruel to confine butterflies, and that no one should make a profit by selling them. What do you think? Is it more, or less, cruel than keeping a cat inside for its entire life, or a rabbit, lizard, hamster, or fish? Should we race horses, sheer sheep for their wool, fish for sport, and have zoos? Some scientists believe that the mass rearing of butterflies is a recipe for the spread of disease. It is true that occasionally butterfly

Butterfly farmers need to grow a lot of host plants to feed their hungry caterpillars. This is giant milkweed.

WELCOME TO Butterfly Dans

Visitors at Butterfly Dan's enjoy a tour of a working butterfly farm, including the caterpillar-rearing room, innovative plant propagation, a butterfly house, sanitation procedures, a gift shop, and maybe even a chance to eat insects! I sampled a few. Will you?

breeders run into trouble with disease, as all farmers do. No breeder wants to sell unhealthy butterflies, or they would soon be out of business. Most have developed the most intricate systems to control disease, and they share it with newcomers anxious to learn.

I have personally met more than 50 butterfly breeders. Every one of them is passionate about butterfly welfare, which incorporates conservation and habitat restoration. They make presentations at schools, lobby local governments to protect wild areas, and set up educational displays at local events. Many inspire the love of nature by opening their farms to the public. I had an opportunity to visit Butterfly Dan's farm in Florida and view his innovative hydroponic gardening techniques for growing host plants, his methods for disease prevention, and various butterflies in all stages of their life cycle. I learned so much while having fun.

Plant propagation.

Eastern black swallowtail.

Eastern Black Swallowtail

The Eastern black swallowtail *Papilio polyxenes* is a common backyard visitor. This butterfly often goes unnoticed because it appears to be solid black, and because it flies quickly. It lays its round yellow eggs on dill, fennel, parsley, carrots, and rue. My day job as a personal fitness trainer takes me to many private gardens. I exercise with older people in their homes. I asked one of them if I could check her dill plants for caterpillars. The owner proudly told me that there were none, just little black worms, which she squished regularly! On another occasion, I went to a client's backyard to check the abundant dill that had seeded itself in the garden from potted dill situated at the edge of the patio. The entire patch was gone! The gardener, not recognizing it as something he had planted, tore all of it out. The first and second instars of the black swallowtail look like little black worms, and people squish them out of fear that they will consume all their herbs. If they would leave them alone, they would never miss the herbs, and they would be rewarded with butterflies and birds.

The first two instars are spiky, but safe to handle.

Most swallowtails,
like this giant swallowtail,
have osmeteria.

Each instar of the eastern black swallowtail looks like a completely different caterpillar! Take out your magnifying glass to see the orange and white spots, and the black spikes of the second instar. Notice the splash of white in the middle, called a saddle, making the caterpillar resemble a bird dropping. That trick keeps many predators away. Those that do attack will be met by the forked **osmeterium**, which most swallowtails use to defend themselves. In addition to looking fierce, the osmeterium emits a foul smell. Wasps will still chew them up for their own larvae back in the nest, and birds will gobble them up and take some home for the chicks.

As the caterpillar grows, it loses its spikes, and its saddle. It is usually green with yellow-spotted black stripes, but you may also find black ones, with yellow-spotted green stripes. They are often mistaken for monarch caterpillars, even though monarchs are black, white, and yellow, and are found only on milkweed.

At this stage, they become vulnerable to the parasitic wasp trogus pennator. This wasp injects an egg right inside the caterpillar. Despite the wasp larva eating its guts out, the caterpillar often remains strong enough to make a chrysalis. My first experience with this parasite was horrific! I was checking the rearing container one morning, when I

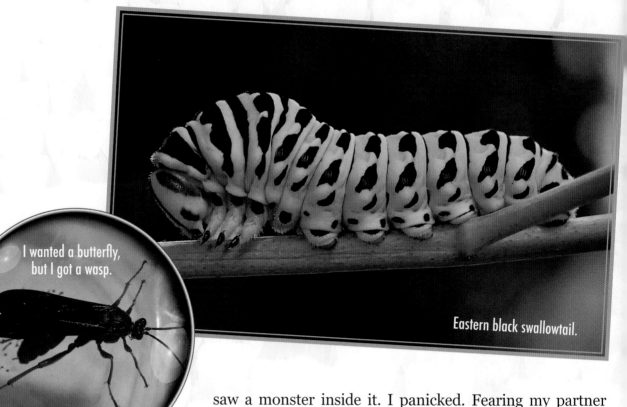

I wanted a butterfly, but I got a wasp.

Eastern black swallowtail.

saw a monster inside it. I panicked. Fearing my partner might see it and cancel her permission to let me use the dining room table as a caterpillar laboratory, I hastily took it outside and let it go. When I regained my composure, I realized I hadn't taken a photo of it. The next time, I had a plan. I learned the secret to getting a clear shot of a flying insect. When I discovered a wasp and an empty chrysalis case, I put their container in the fridge for 15 minutes. When I took it out, the wasp was too cold to fly. I took it outside, got my photos, and in minutes the sun had warmed it up to flying temperature. Off it went. Some people kill parasites. In fact, a lot of people do. They like the idea of sparing an insect that they enjoy for its colour, like a butterfly, the fate of being eaten from the inside out by an unattractive parasitic fly or wasp. Can you think of examples of animals that kill other animals for food? Which do you root for, the predator, or the prey? Why? (I root for the hawk, but it's not easy.)

Eastern black swallowtail caterpillars never seem to be in a hurry to eat, resting for long periods during the day. If you are used to watching monarchs, which chomp voraciously throughout the day, you might think your swallowtails are not thriving. They eat for about three weeks before they are ready to sculpt a chrysalis. When I saw my first one

It took 45 minutes for this caterpillar to complete its sling. In just 11 days it was about to start its life as a butterfly.

dripping green fluid into a watery load of brown frass, I was sure it was not going to make it. That would be a sign of poisoning in a monarch.

Just when I was fearing the worst, the caterpillar spun an elaborate sling. Through various contortions, it managed to get its head through it, thereby suspending itself from the twig to which it had earlier attached its rear **claspers**. I later learned that the watery excrement meant the caterpillar was **purging**, which is normal for a black swallowtail.

For two weeks, big changes were going on inside the still-looking chrysalis. The caterpillar was giving way to new wings, antennae, long legs and **brush feet**, complex eyes, and circulatory and reproductive systems. Finally, the **pupal case** became transparent, and I could see the butterfly inside. That's how I knew it would emerge the next day. I watched in amazement as the case cracked open and the new

In 10 days or so, this swallowtail will be ready to emerge.

The swallowtail is shedding its skin for the last time, revealing the chrysalis it has been making inside.

butterfly squeezed itself out. Immediately, it pumped fluid from its round abdomen into its crumpled wings, which quickly expanded. I waited an hour for them to partially dry, then offered my finger. At this point, the butterfly is strong enough to walk and starts to slowly exercise its wings. It is not yet ready to fly.

This is a photographer's dream come true. You can direct the butterfly to light on anything you want: your nose, an object, or any flower in your garden. It will hang on tight, allowing you to take hundreds of photos. This is your time to experiment with your camera. Try the different buttons, zoom in and out, get closer, change the angles, and pay attention to the background. You may want to make a print or plaque of your best one and hang it on the wall.

The eastern black swallowtail is found throughout southern Canada, most of the eastern and mid-western United States west to the Rocky Mountains, and southwest into Arizona, Mexico, and northern South America. Throughout most of their range, they have two broods every year. Late season chrysalises spend the entire winter hibernating. When I first put my September chrysalises in my unheated garage until spring, I was certain they could not possibly survive. They do, of course, even when they are outside surrounded by snow. As the temperature rises, the chrysalises mature, and the swallowtails emerge, just as the dandelions begin to bloom.

Swallowtails are among the many butterflies and moths that do not migrate. Instead, they spend the winter as a pupae. For butterflies, that means they "hibernate" as a chrysalis; moth pupae protect themselves in a cocoon. The swallowtail caterpillar finds a protected place, usually on a tree, to make its chrysalis. If it doesn't get eaten, and hasn't been parasitized, it will emerge when it warms up in the spring. It will survive months of freezing temperatures. They are among the first butterflies we see in spring, because ... they were here all along. Those common little white butterflies, called cabbage whites, as well as sulphurs, are examples of other butterflies we see in early spring, because they have spent the winter in their chrysalids.

It is a magical feeling to watch this tiny creature take its first flight.

If you decide to raise eastern black swallowtails, and you live where it snows, you'll need to store your late season chrysalises in a very cold place. If your garage is well insulated, you may enter it one winter day to find a butterfly has emerged too soon. While it would be fun to care for it as a pet, we really want it to complete its life mission by breeding during the spring.

In the meadow, eastern black swallowtails lay their eggs on Queen Anne's lace, golden alexander and wild parsnip.

LOCATION MAP
OF THE EASTERN BLACK SWALLOWTAIL

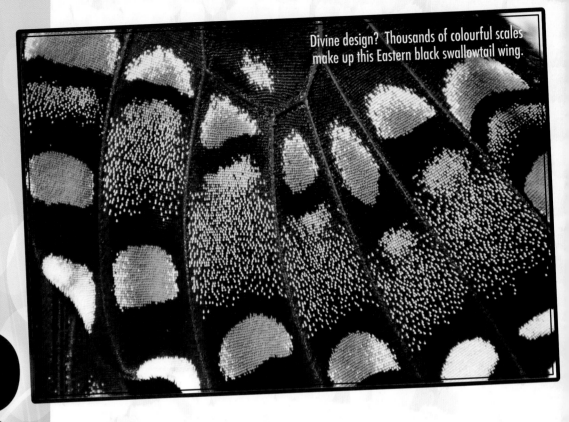
Divine design? Thousands of colourful scales make up this Eastern black swallowtail wing.

The Spirituality of Butterflies

In 2019, the world wept as Notre Dame Cathedral in Paris burned. Construction began in the 12th century and took about 100 years. In one week, donors contributed $1.5 billion for its restoration. Why? Because the building incorporates history, culture, religion, art, spirit, music, genius, architecture, and beauty. Are butterflies any less worthy of saving? Are they not all this, and more?

Butterflies are living art. Thousands of scales come together to form meticulous tapestries that actually come to you. You need only look out the window, or be still in the meadow, to marvel at their beauty. Or spend a magical hour at a butterfly conservatory, where vibrant butterflies from all over the world may land on you at any moment.

Butterflies have symbolic meaning in cultures around the globe. In China, they represent young love, long life, immortality, marriage, and the undying bond between lovers. For Christians, butterflies are a symbol of rebirth, or resurrection. The ancient Greeks believed the butterfly was a human soul, released from a deceased body. Many indigenous

Day of the Dead celebrations in Mexico.

Mexicans believe that butterflies carry the souls of their departed. They celebrate the Day of the Dead just as the monarch butterflies arrive in Mexico. And they keep alive their legend that if you whisper a wish to a butterfly, it will take it to the Great Spirit, who will grant your wish in gratitude for setting the butterfly free.

We see butterflies displayed every-where as a symbol of beauty, freedom, good health, and happiness. Companies feature them to indicate that their products are environmentally friendly. Organizations for the deaf use a monarch as their logo, as monarchs are deaf. In the United States, Dreamers have adopted it as a symbol to advocate for immigrant rights. For addicts, cancer survivors, mourners, and others who experience illness or loss, butterflies are a symbol of recovery. Countless others see them as representing hope,

The awe of connecting with another life.

strength, tenacity, healing, creativity, and transformation. We can all be inspired by the humble yet amazing caterpillar, which struggles out of its skin many times before hiding in a dark place, to be reinvented as a free-flying, dazzling superstar.

In her book *The Butterfly Club: "Is That You?"* butterfly spirituality expert Phyllis Calvey has documented dozens of real-life experiences of butterflies bringing messages from the departed. After every presentation, audience members line up to recount their own experiences. Others post them to her website. Hundreds of testimonials can also be found at butterflywebsite.com. The stories have one thing in common. Each person believes, and feels, the presence of a loved one who has died.

What if everything you are going through right now is preparing you for a dream bigger than you can imagine?

–Ranae A. Sauter

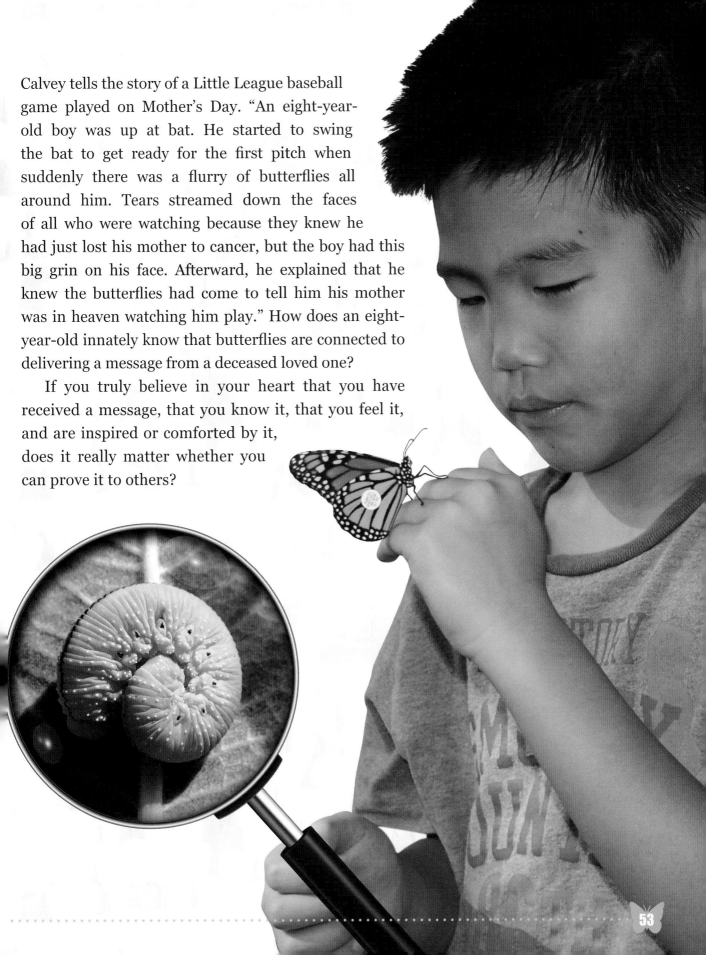

Calvey tells the story of a Little League baseball game played on Mother's Day. "An eight-year-old boy was up at bat. He started to swing the bat to get ready for the first pitch when suddenly there was a flurry of butterflies all around him. Tears streamed down the faces of all who were watching because they knew he had just lost his mother to cancer, but the boy had this big grin on his face. Afterward, he explained that he knew the butterflies had come to tell him his mother was in heaven watching him play." How does an eight-year-old innately know that butterflies are connected to delivering a message from a deceased loved one?

If you truly believe in your heart that you have received a message, that you know it, that you feel it, and are inspired or comforted by it, does it really matter whether you can prove it to others?

Question mark.

Question Mark

Yes, question mark is the name of a butterfly. You might confuse it with the similar-looking eastern comma butterfly. Truly, even scientists who give names to butterflies have a sense of humour. If you look carefully, you will find a small question mark on the wing of a question mark butterfly *Polygonia interrogationis*, and a small comma on the wing of a comma butterfly *Polygonia comma*.

The question mark ranges across the eastern two-thirds of the United States, up into southern Canada, and south to Mexico. You can find it in woodlands, swamps, parks, and especially in gardens that you create at home, or in your community, that provide it with the habitat it needs to complete its life cycle.

You may spot a question mark on a sunny spring day, while the snow is still on the ground. They feed on tree sap or probe the ground for dead animal bits, dung, or freshly thawed rotting fruit. Later in the season, if these preferred foods are not available, they will nectar on flowers. Will a late winter storm kill them? Where have they spent the winter?

Adult question marks, like mourning cloaks, commas, and tortoiseshell butterflies, hide under tree bark, in hollow logs, or in crevices during the winter. They may emerge on a warm, sunny day, then go back into hiding if the weather turns cold again. You can invite them to your yard by adding overripe bananas, melons, or rotting apples to your compost heap, or hanging them from your bird feeder pole.

The female lays her green-ridged eggs singly, in groups, or in stacks on or near nettles, elm, hackberry, and hop vines. The eggs hatch in about five days. With each moult, the caterpillar will sprout a different-looking set of spikes, designed to slow down its predators. Even more fascinating is that there are so many variations that even two caterpillars in the same instar can look very different. As the caterpillar grows, it stitches up a leaf of its host plant to conceal itself when it rests. I search for these folded leaves, knowing that there is a prize inside. On nettles, there is usually a red admiral, comma, or question mark caterpillar. Sometimes, a predator will have discovered the hideaway. Other times, another insect is using the same strategy; sometimes ... even a ... spider. I open the leaf slowly, with my gloves on, to keep from getting stung. I prepare to confront my fear of spiders.

A folded leaf means there's a surprise inside.

The caterpillar stitched the leaf so that it could hide. It repaired it after I peeked inside.

While the spikes of many caterpillars can sting, this caterpillar is safe to handle.

Yuck! It can be gross to see parasitic larvae killing your caterpillar, but the wasp that injected its eggs here completed its mission.

When ready to make its chrysalis, the question mark caterpillar will attach itself to a sturdy leaf or twig, then hang in a "J" shape for about a day. A week later, you will have an opportunity to see how it protects itself as an adult. At rest, with wings closed, it disappears by disguising itself as a dead leaf. Its rusty orange and brown wings, spotted with black, are visible only when open.

Unless it is part of the overwintering generation, an adult question mark will live up to three weeks, if it escapes the lizards, birds, praying mantises, and other predators that patrol its habitat, looking for dinner.

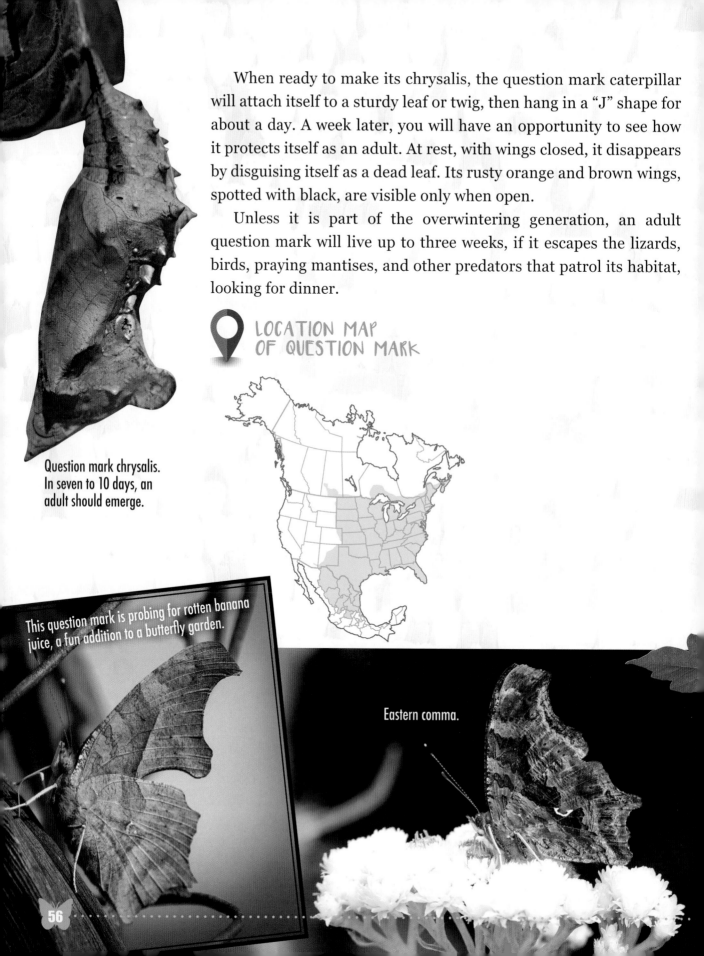

Question mark chrysalis. In seven to 10 days, an adult should emerge.

LOCATION MAP
OF QUESTION MARK

This question mark is probing for rotten banana juice, a fun addition to a butterfly garden.

Eastern comma.

Being Safe in the Meadow

Before heading out to explore the meadow, woods, or wetland, there are a few things you need to be aware of. Plants secrete fluids that can hurt you, and, as you know, bugs bite. A few simple precautions will keep you safe, so don't be thinking these are reasons to avoid going outside. I didn't know any of this for the first 30 years of my nature treks, and none of my injuries lasted for more than a couple of hours.

Your best defence against just about everything is long sleeves, and long pants tucked into your socks. This will protect you from ticks, stinging nettles, poison oak, and poison ivy. Gloves will protect your hands. You don't want the nettles to sting, and you don't want plant fluids, especially the milky white sap from milkweed, to get into your eyes. That happens when you touch your eyes after handling plants that are leaking fluids or sap.

I must admit that I don't always follow my own advice. I don't like to be hot, and I am willing to pay for wearing shorts with the occasional red ant bite (hurts for about an hour), or a slight brush with the nettles (hurts for several hours). I look carefully to avoid poison ivy. I check for ticks throughout the day, and more thoroughly when I get home. I swat the mosquitoes or apply a hint of insect repellant. If I get plant fluids on my hands, I clean them with the damp cloth that I usually bring along or wash them in the river. If neither of those options is available, I am very careful not to touch my eyes, or my forehead, until I have a chance to wash my hands.

While most tick bites are harmless, some are serious. It's best to tell your doctor if you discover a tick attached to your skin.

These are the stinging nettles stingers. Surprisingly, people who have grown up harvesting these plants develop an immunity.

Stinging nettles.

There are only three leaves on each stem.

Cecropia

I know this book is called *5 Butterflies*, but moths deserve at least one chapter. Moths often get a bad rap. The ones we usually see are grey or brown, flying in circles around porch lights. Occasionally one makes it into the house. They don't bite or sting. Are they really a problem? Our parents didn't like them when they chewed holes in their wool sweaters, but there are only two species that do that, and they can be deterred with moth balls. And some people don't like to see nibble marks on their plants, or on the leaves of their trees. Doug Tallamy, author of *Bringing Nature Home*, has a solution to that problem. He recommends taking 10 giants steps away from the foliage!

One day, while walking in the ravine, I came across huge nests of wiggly, cream-coloured caterpillars. Most people would consider them unsightly. I brought a few home, along with a stash of leaves from the tree I found them on, to watch them grow. From my field guide, I identified them as army worms. To my delight, they blossomed into exquisite, friendly, elongated white moths with black spots, called spindle ermines.

You can learn to love moths by hanging a light-coloured bed sheet outside at night, with a light shining on it. Moths will be drawn to the light and will cling to the sheet. First thing next morning, race out to see what you've "caught." What a fun way to start your day. The moths will leave when they are ready, but you will have had time to photograph and identify them. Perhaps you will keep a pregnant female for a day, so that she can lay eggs for you during that time. Of course, you will have to research what they eat (their host plant) before doing this.

Spindle ermine caterpillars and spindle ermine adult.

One of my favourite moths is the cecropia *Hyalophora cecropia*. Cecropias are the largest moths native to North America. They are part of the silk moth family, which includes luna, promethea, and polyphemus moths. The famous member of this family is the Chinese silkworm *Bombyx mori*. It has been farmed for thousands of years in China to provide the beautiful silk used in garments.

Most people will never see an adult cecropia. That's because, throughout much of its breeding range, it will have only one brood, and it will live only one week! Adult cecropias never eat; in fact, they have no mouth parts. Their only job is to reproduce. The day a female emerges in spring, it will emit strong **pheromones** (chemicals), which the male will detect from up to a mile away. They fly only at night. During the day, they rest on tree trunks, as do other silk moths. Females lay rows of two to six eggs on both sides of the leaves of small host trees or shrubs. If you have raised butterflies, you might think that your cecropia eggs are not viable, because they are hard, and they take 10 to 14 days to hatch.

You may, however, be lucky enough to spot a caterpillar. Each instar is excitingly different. From the third instar, it is green, and with each moult comes a new festive array of spikes and bobbles, called tubercles. It is hard to imagine how the caterpillar could crawl out of that skin, even when you see it happening. It takes five to seven weeks before it is ready to make its pupa. Often, it will leave its host tree to search out the most protected spot. This is a good time, in late summer, to look for the huge caterpillar, as it might be racing on the ground or over a rock. It is likely finished eating, but if you want to take it home you should identify it with your caterpillar field guide. Examples of these can be found in the Resources page at the back of this book.

It will need a few twigs from its host tree, with fresh leaves on them. After perhaps taking a few more bites, the caterpillar stitches the leaves together with its silk. The process is entrancing to watch. When the structure is strong enough, the caterpillar will moult for the final time, exposing the pupa it has been forming inside. In the meantime, the cocoon will have hardened. If you wanted to peek at the pupa, you would need a pair of good scissors. That's how tough the cocoon is! It would be hard for a predator to chew through it. As you try to cut it, the pupa will wiggle in an attempt to scare you off. I put this pupa (page 62) back in its cocoon.

Newly hatched cecropia.

Fresh out of its skin!

Even the spiracles are a work of art on this striking cecropia.

Every summer, I raise many species of moths. If they make a cocoon late in the summer, I put each species in a separate, slightly ventilated container and label each with its name and the date. I then store them for the winter in my unheated garage, moving them to a porch in early spring. I put them in a place where I will pass by them daily. I don't want to be surprised (again) by discovering a dead moth in a cage in the garage. That happens when the moth emerges without my noticing. In the wild, the pupae generally survive the cold and snow to finish maturing when the temperature rises.

The new moth will secrete juices to dissolve a hole in its tough cocoon. It will then crawl out and begin to pump up its wings. Slowly and methodically, it opens and closes them, displaying its vibrant grey and orange colours. The female's abdomen is swollen with her numerous large eggs. Her antennae are thin, unlike the wide feathery antennae of the male. If you have raised the cecropias from eggs found in close proximity, you need to store the cocoons in individual containers. If you don't, the siblings will mate the day they emerge, like mine did. Mating among siblings increases the likelihood of mutation.

Each cecropia instar looks different from the one before.

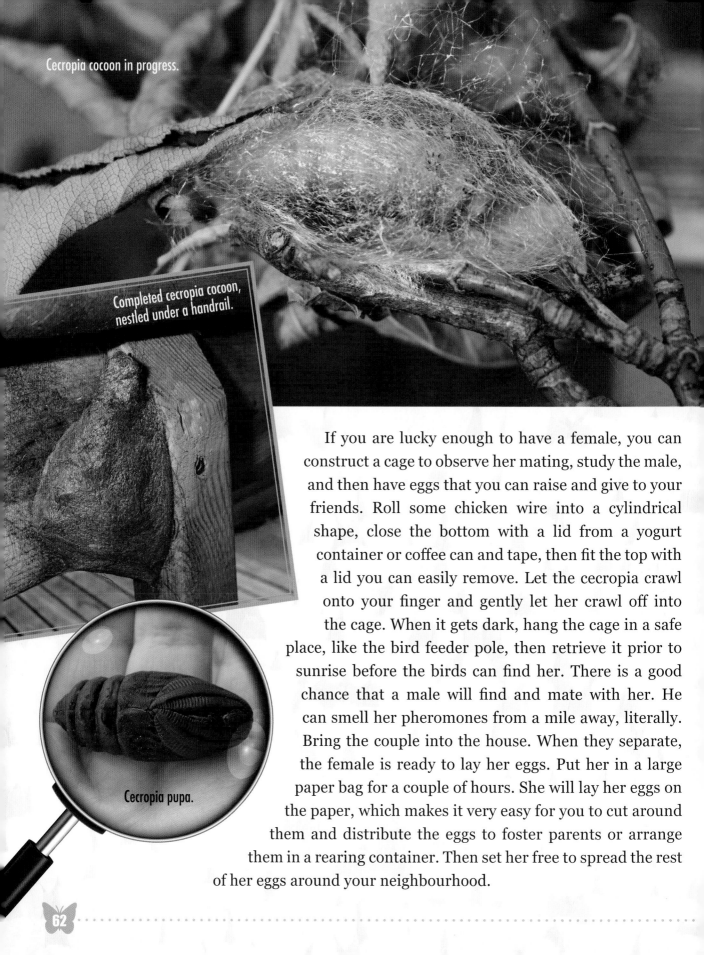

Cecropia cocoon in progress.

Completed cecropia cocoon, nestled under a handrail.

Cecropia pupa.

If you are lucky enough to have a female, you can construct a cage to observe her mating, study the male, and then have eggs that you can raise and give to your friends. Roll some chicken wire into a cylindrical shape, close the bottom with a lid from a yogurt container or coffee can and tape, then fit the top with a lid you can easily remove. Let the cecropia crawl onto your finger and gently let her crawl off into the cage. When it gets dark, hang the cage in a safe place, like the bird feeder pole, then retrieve it prior to sunrise before the birds can find her. There is a good chance that a male will find and mate with her. He can smell her pheromones from a mile away, literally. Bring the couple into the house. When they separate, the female is ready to lay her eggs. Put her in a large paper bag for a couple of hours. She will lay her eggs on the paper, which makes it very easy for you to cut around them and distribute the eggs to foster parents or arrange them in a rearing container. Then set her free to spread the rest of her eggs around your neighbourhood.

The cecropia male's antennae are feathery. The female has a large abdomen full of eggs, and sleek antennae.

Female cecropias will lay their eggs on various trees and shrubs, including sugar maple, wild cherries, plums, apples, alder, birch, box elder, dogwoods, willows, and lilacs.

Cecropia moths can be found east of the Rocky Mountains in the United States and Canada.

LOCATION MAP
OF CECROPIA

There are about 160,000 species of moths in the world, with at least 5,000 occurring in Canada.

The Planet Needs Your Help

YOUR TIME AS A CATERPILLAR HAS EXPIRED. YOUR WINGS ARE READY.

All over the world, animals and plants are going extinct at the rate of dozens a day. At this pace, more than half of all species on Earth could be lost by 2100. This includes mammals, reptiles, and insects. It would be easy for us to feel helpless in the midst of such devastating numbers.

The encouraging news is that each of us can make a real difference in conserving wildlife, right in our own region. We will be able to see the results of our efforts flying, buzzing, crawling, and blooming all around us.

CREATE AND RESTORE HABITAT

What land can you influence? Your garden, the garden around your apartment, your club, your place of worship, your cousin's place, your grandparents' home, or your school? Get a group together. Organize a planting party. Invite the press.

Contact politicians to ask them to take the Mayor's Pledge. Created by the US National Wildlife Federation, this program has expanded to include Mexico and Canada. Municipalities that take the pledge commit to implementing at least three of 25 recommended action items designed to create monarch habitat and engage residents in educational and conservation projects. Any action that is good for monarch butterflies is good for all butterflies and, indeed, all insects and their predators.

Contact politicians to ask them to install butterfly gardens at police stations, fire halls, community centres, government offices, and other suitable locations.

Convert most of your lawn to butterfly gardens. Display signage so that your neighbours will learn. Certification is also a good way to connect with the issuing organizations and to see how many others have established gardens like yours: nwf.org/Garden-for-Wildlife/Certify, nababutterfly.com/butterfly-garden-certification-program, monarchwatch.org

A pollinator garden on a boulevard.

Don't kill your leps! Leps is the casual word enthusiasts use for butterflies and moths.

❀ Don't squish the tiny insects living in your garden. Most of them are native and important for the ecosystem. Many of them are caterpillars, which will become gorgeous adults.

❀ When you are exploring the meadow, try to stay on the trails. Many butterflies and moths spend their egg, caterpillar, or larval stage on the meadow or forest floor, often under leaf litter. If you step on it, you kill it.

❀ Don't rake your leaves in the fall. It's where so many insects spend the winter.

❀ Above all, try not to use insecticides. Enjoy your insects, instead.

If you find a live insect on store-bought vegetables, celebrate! It means they haven't been overdosed with poison.

Volunteer with your local naturalist group to plant and maintain butterfly gardens. Do you live in an area regulated by a Homeowners Association? Start a revolution! Many HOA's require homeowners to keep a perfect, well-manicured lawn, with flowers no higher than a couple of feet. This rules out many native plants. You can start to change the conversation. Write a letter to your local newspaper. Did you know that Letters to the Editor is one of the most-read features? Another way to get attention is replace a few square feet of your front lawn with native plants, then, if you get a letter telling you to cut them down, call the newspaper. Prepare four or five short, clear sentences to explain why you are creating habitat.

Even a portion of your lawn can be converted to a thriving pollinator garden.

In Canada, the same outdated front lawn rules are enforced by condominium associations, and even by the neighbours on residential streets. Condominium and city bylaws prescribe a height limit that is shorter than most native plants. If you live in a condominium, encourage a parent to become a board member. Educate the others to change the rules about what residents are allowed to plant. If you live on a street make sure you get along with your neighbours. The City enforces its bylaws only when someone registers a complaint. Add small labels on sticks or painted onto rocks to identify your plants, in addition to a sign from any of the many conservation organizations that will certify your garden. Explain your habitat to passersby. That way, your garden will look intentional. Your neighbours won't complain to the City. They might even follow your example and replace their own front lawn with beautiful, productive native flowers.

RAISE CATERPILLARS

I encourage you to plant host plants, like milkweed, or search for eggs and caterpillars in the wild so that you can marvel over their development every day.

Use the resources at the back of this book to learn which butterflies live in your region, and which, mostly native, plants you will need to attract them. You can also scour nearby wild areas. If you find a caterpillar, bring it home with a good supply of the leaves you found it on. Take just one or two caterpillars.

During your visits to the meadows, woodlands, and ravines, you will discover the thousands of tiny creatures, as well as their larger predators, that make these places their homes. By actually caring for a few of them, you will be awestruck by their complexity, tenacity, growth, and transformation. Then, something wonderful will happen. You will start to care about them. You will want to protect their habitat. If it were up to Big Business and Big Government, every square inch of land would be paved over or doused with chemicals. Only your love for wildlife can preserve insects for the next generations, and along with them, clean air, water, trees, animals, birds ...

TEACH

❀ Teach wherever you can, to one person, or to a crowd. Clubs, camps, retreats, retirement residences, and social groups are always looking for speakers. Yes, with just a little experience raising caterpillars, you can be a teacher, and you will relish being the authority. Contact me at monarchcrusader@gmail.com to receive my free slide presentation and script.

❀ Organize a butterfly festival or event at your place of worship, conservation area, school, farm, or local business. Monarch Joint Venture has published a complete how-to manual, which you can find in the Resources.

❀ Exhibit a teaching table at your local fair, market, or nature conference.

❀ Raise the caterpillars you find. Post your photos on social media. Display your rearing containers to friends, family members, and classmates. Give away caterpillars and teach others to raise them. Give away chrysalises.

❀ Lead a caterpillar hunt and nature walk.

❀ Paint murals of butterflies, moths, and meadows in public places (with permission).

You are the expert, and people will get excited from what you show them.

CONTRIBUTE

❀ Contribute to organizations that conserve butterflies.

❀ Support projects, like movies, that will spread awareness of the plight of butterflies. Some examples of crowd-funded movies are *Beauty on the Wing*, directed by Kim Smith, and *The Butterfly Trees*, directed by Kay Milam.

❀ Organize a fundraiser for your favourite organization or to build a butterfly garden.

BECOME A CITIZEN SCIENTIST

Did you know that your observations can be reviewed by scientists for analysis? Scientists don't have the time, manpower, or money to visit every state and province to investigate wildlife. Your observations allow them to get a picture of regional insect populations.

ebutterfly

Anyone, anytime, anywhere in North America (soon to be expanded to the Caribbean and Central America) can submit their observations of butterflies and moths at every stage. These data provide scientists, land managers, conservationists, naturalists, and students with information about butterfly distribution and abundance. Observations can be posted to e-butterfly.org

iNaturalist

Use any of your devices to post observations, from the rarest butterfly to the most common backyard weed. Your findings are shared with scientists, and you can connect and learn from other naturalists! inaturalist.org

Participate in a butterfly count

The North American Butterfly Association organizes a Butterfly Count Program in the United States, Canada, and Mexico initiated by the Xerces Society in 1975. Each of the approximately 450 counts consists of a compilation of all butterflies observed at sites within a 24-kilometre (15-mile) diameter count circle in a one-day period. The annually published reports provide a tremendous amount of information about the geographical distribution and relative population sizes of the species counted. Comparisons of the results across years can be used to monitor changes in butterfly populations and study the effects of weather and habitat change on North American butterflies. butterflies.naba.org/how-to-participate-in-a-butterfly-count/, butterflywebsite.com/butterfly-counts.cfm

Actual Wingspan

American lady	1¾ to 2⅛ inches	44 to 54 mm
Question mark	2⅜ to 2⅝ inches	60 to 67 mm
Black swallowtail	2⅝ to 3½ inches	67 to 89mm
Monarch	3 ½ to 4 inches	89 to 102mm
Cecropia	4 5/16 to 5 ⅞ inches	110 to 150 mm

Epilogue

What Does Your Future Look Like?

How are you feeling today? Did you jump out of bed this morning, filled with enthusiasm, ready to tackle the day? Did you wonder whether you would have enough hours to complete everything you wanted to do? Or were you tired, bored, and unhappy?

Do you suffer from back, neck, or wrist pain? Are you moody or depressed?

Most teens are aware that the first thing they do in the morning and the last thing before going to sleep is check their cellphone; during the day, about every nine minutes. They also know that screen addiction affects their ability to do homework, cross the street safely, listen to a lecture, or even talk to a friend. They may suffer from anxiety and isolation, with or without their devices. They want to break free but cannot.

If you can find your passion outside, we will all be healthier and happier. Will you fall in love with birds, fungi, rushing water, the

Even in the centre of a city, you can observe some of nature's most incredible stories. Salmon swim up the polluted Don River in Toronto to **spawn** at the spot where they hatched.

scent of pine needles? Will you discover that your most creative thoughts magically enter your head while you walk a trail? Will you be overcome by a feeling of peace and a connection to all living things? While my greatest love is nurturing caterpillars, the search for them has opened up all of those rewards for me. I am rarely bored. Outfitted with a specimen container and a camera, I spend hours on end scouring my yard, my potted plants, the roadside, meadow, or ravine for tiny creatures to examine. My dining room table becomes a living zoo, each caterpillar requiring my loving care. Over the winter, I organize my photos to make plaques, presentations, and greeting cards. Additionally, I have more energy, I have control of my weight, and, more often than not, gratitude replaces worrying about trivial things.

Your love of nature will inspire you to speak to your politicians about conservation; then one day become the politician who writes the laws. You might write letters to businesses, asking them to become more environmentally friendly, then start your own "green" company. All of tomorrow's leaders must be convinced that nature is not "over there," but that we actually breathe it, drink it, and enjoy it.

Discover it.
Love it.
Protect it.

Other Caterpillars You Can Raise

The caterpillars on this page are all safe to handle.

73

Resources

RECOMMENDED WEB SITES

<u>gardenswithwings.com</u> Just type in your US zip code, and you'll get beautiful photos of all the butterflies you can attract. One click then takes you to the host and nectar plants you'll need, and the next click takes you to complete life cycle information!

<u>xerces.org</u> Spend some time browsing this comprehensive website to find webinars, workshops, volunteer opportunities, a wide range of printable fact sheets, and just about everything you need to know for your pollinator project. The Xerces Society for Invertebrate Conservation

<u>butterfly-fun-facts.com</u> Plain language answers to your questions about butterfly and moth raising, disease, predators, host plants, gardening and more.

<u>butterfliesandmoths.org</u> is your one stop data base including range maps, photos, and life cycle.

<u>raisingbutterflies.org</u> For the advanced student, life cycle photographs of more than 100 butterfly species, dozens of how-to videos, a store to purchase rearing containers, and a direct link to Ask the Expert!

<u>monarchwatch.org</u> You can buy monarch tags here.

<u>butterflywebsite.com</u> Lists of butterfly festivals and butterfly houses world wide.

<u>todocanada.ca</u> To find Canadian festivals, search for 'butterfly festival'.

<u>monarchjointventure.org/images/uploads/documents/FINAL_Monarch_Festival_Planning_Guide.pdf</u> Everything you need to know to plan your very own butterfly festival.

RECOMMENDED FIELD GUIDES

Allen, Thomas J., Jim P. Brock, and Jeffrey Glassberg. 2005. *Caterpillars in the Field and Garden: A Field Guide to the Butterfly Caterpillars of North America.* Oxford University Press.

Amy Bartlett Wright. 2003. *Peterson First Guide to Caterpillars of North America Paperback.* 2nd edition. Houghton Mifflin Harcourt.

Beadle, David and Seabrooke Leckie. 2012. *Peterson Field Guide to Moths of Northeastern North America*. New York, NY: Houghton Mifflin Harcourt.

Brock, Jim P. and Kenn Kaufman. 2006. *Field Guide to Butterflies of North America (Kaufman Filed Guides)*. Boston, MA: Houghton Mifflin Harcourt.

Leckie, Seabrooke and David Beadle. 2018. *Peterson Field Guide to Moths of Southeastern North America*. New York, NY: Houghton Mifflin Harcourt.

Wagner, David L. 2005. *Caterpillars of Eastern North America: A Guide to Identification and Natural History*. Princeton, NJ: Princeton University Press.

RECOMMENDED BOOKS

Raising Butterflies in the Garden Brenda Dziedzic Firefly Books 2019. This book features more than 500 colour photographs showing the life cycles of 40 common butterflies and moths -- from egg to adult -- as well as the host and nectar plants they rely on.

The Secret Lives of Backyard Bugs Judy Burris and Wayne Richards Storey Publishing 2011 While hunting for caterpillars, you will discover a world of insects. This book explains their life cycles in conversation language, with hundreds of stunning photographs.

Milkweeds, Monarchs and More: A Field Guide to the Invertebrate Community in the Milkweed Patch Enlarged Edition Ba Rea, Karen Oberhauser and Michael A Quin, Bas Relief LLC 2010 Brilliantly illustrated, this book is a more academic, scientific, easy to use, story of the insects in the meadow. I especially like that each one is classified by role, with a simple colour code, as herbivore, nectivore, predator, parasite, or scavenger.

How To Raise Monarch Butterflies A Step-by-Step Guide for Kids Carol Pasternak Firefly Books 2012 Loved by young people and adults alike, this beautifully photographed introduction to raising butterflies will turn anyone into an instant expert. Perfect for explaining your hobby to family and friends.

My, Oh My - a Butterfly! Tish Rabe Random House Children's Books 2007 It's hard to believe that this Dr. Seuss style book can teach the life cycle of butterflies and moths with silly illustrations and rhymes, but it does. In no time even the youngest child will be able to say 'proboscis', and know what it does!

Bibliography

https://species-registry.canada.ca/index-en.html#/species?taxonomyId=8&sortBy=commonNameSort&sortDirection=asc&pageSize=10

https://monarchjointventure.org/images/uploads/presentations/garcia_serrano.pdf This is the source of info for Fondo Monarca. Money given to ejidos.

https://www.wwf.org.mx/que_hacemos/programas/mariposa_monarca/fondo_para_la_conservacion/ description of Fondo Monarca

https://www.nationalgeographic.com/animals/article/animals-endangered-back-from-brink-conservation-news

https://www.nationalgeographic.com/animals/article/why-insect-populations-are-plummeting-and-why-it-matters

http://butterfly-lady.com/native-american-legends-of-the-butterfly/?fbclid=IwAR33G0HiMX1b8ZEd7wmYZmbIZclh2WreXWkxfrssrTBbBhFA_LzrzmGfBxg

https://www.naturalhistorycuriosities.com/insects/the-sustainable-evolution-of-butterfly-breeding/

https://www.sciencedirect.com/science/article/pii/S0006320718313636?via%3Dihub former loggers now breeding butterflies!

https://news.mongabay.com/2019/02/butterfly-business-insect-farmers-help-conserve-east-african-forests/

http://erepository.uonbi.ac.ke/handle/11295/19353#:~:text=The%20farming%20of%20butterflies%20in,otherwise%20threatened%20from%20over%20exploitation

https://www.sciencedirect.com/science/article/abs/pii/S0006320718313636?via%3Dihub

https://www.nrcs.usda.gov/wps/portal/nrcs/detail/ct/technical/ecoscience/invasive/?cid=nrcs142p2_011124

Photo Credits

Images are copyright Carol Pasternak except

Front cover
Question Mark - Courtesy of Anna Nitschke
  Author head shot - Courtesy of Audrey Kouyoumdjian

Page 4
Monarchs nectaring - Courtesy of John Blair

Page 6
Beautiful wood nymph caterpillar courtesy of Don Scallen

Page 7
Monarch range map - Courtesy of Fred Miller and Patty Bigner, GardensWithWings.com

Page 17
Parasitized chrysalis - Courtesy of Rob Wood

Page 18
Girl watching caterpillar - Courtesy of David Ringer

Page 27
Students with money, and students packing rocks. Courtesy of Estela Romero.

Page 29
Shutterstock photo

Page 30
Shutterstock photo

Page 32
Vireo feeding chicks - Courtesy of Doug Tallamy

Page 33
In The Zone With permission from Carolinian Canada caroliniancanada.ca

Page 33
Certified Butterfly Garden. With permission from North American Butterfly Association naba.org

Page 37
American lady range map - Courtesy of Fred Miller and Patty Bigner, GardensWithWings.com

Page 39
Taking photos - Courtesy of Audrey Kouyoumdjian

Page 41
Chrysalids and cocoons - Courtesy of Kurtis Herperger butterflygardens.com

Page 43
Butterfly Dan's - Courtesy of Audrey Kouyoumdjian

Page 42
Monarch in envelope - Courtesy of Edith Smith butterfly-fun-facts.com

Page 45
Swallowtail osmeterium - Courtesy of Kelly Ballard joyfulbutterfly.com

Page 49
Eastern black swallowtail range map - Courtesy of Fred Miller and Patty Bigner, GardensWithWings.com

Page 51
Day of the Dead altar - Courtesy of Sean Doorly
  Day of the Dead parade - Courtesy of Dylan Wong

Page 54
Question mark - Courtesy of Vasura Jayaweera

Page 56
Eastern comma - Courtesy of Brenda Dziedzic
  Question mark on banana - Courtesy of Jill Streit Murphy
  Question mark range map - Courtesy of Fred Miller and Patty Bigner, GardensWithWings.com

Page 57
Shutterstock photos

Page 63
Cecropia range map - Courtesy of Fred Miller and Patty Bigner, GardensWithWings.com

Page 64
Shutterstock photo

Page 66
Native plant garden - Courtesy of Janet Allen ourhabitatgarden.org

Page 68
Cameron teaching - Courtesy of Lisa Carriere

Page 70
Question mark - Courtesy of Anna Nitschke

Page 73
Teresa sphinx - Courtesy of Debra Madere

Page 73
Asteroid and white streaked prominent - Courtesy of Andy Wyatt

Glossary

A

Adult: the final developmental stage of an organism. In Lepidoptera, it is the butterfly or moth.

B

Biophilia: a desire to commune with nature

Brood: a generation of young creatures

Brush feet: reduced forelegs used to help fuse the two parts of the proboscis when the butterfly emerges from the pupal case

C

Chrysalis: the pupa of a butterfly. The developmental stage between caterpillar and adult.

Claspers: the appendages at the end of the male's abdomen. They are used by butterfly caterpillars to secure themselves to a surface from which they can hang while making their chrysalis. Also used by males to hold females while mating.

Cremaster: the small sticklike structure the newly forming chrysalis uses to secure itself to its silk pad

Cuticle: caterpillar skin

E

Eclose: to hatch, used for a butterfly emerging from its chrysalis

Ecotourism: tourism to places having unspoiled natural resources, with minimal impact on the environment being a primary concern

Ecozone: an area with a particular type of natural environment. The ecozones of Canada consist of 15 land and five water zones.

F

Fauna: the animals of a particular region

Flora: the plants of a particular region

Forests for Monarchs: an organization working to reforest both the Monarch Biosphere Reserve and badly degraded land owned by indigenous communities, ejidos, and farmers. See forestsformonarchs.org

Frass: the excrement of caterpillars

G

Glassine: the semi-transparent material commonly used to package breakfast cereals and stamps

H

Habitat: a place that is natural for the life and growth of an organism

Hortophilia: the desire to interact with, manage, and tend nature

Host: a plant that can be eaten by a caterpillar, or an egg or caterpillar from which a parasite feeds

I

Insectivore: a plant or animal that eats insects

Instar: the developmental stage of a caterpillar before its first moult, in between moults, or after its last moult

L

Larva: the caterpillar stage, plural larvae

Lepidoptera: an order of insects that comprises butterflies and moths

M

Metamorphosis: the process of transformation from egg to adult butterfly or moth

Monarch Butterfly Fund: an organization that focuses on habitat conservation, scientific research and monitoring, outreach and education, and sustainable development in and around the monarch biosphere. See monarchconservation.org

Monarch sanctuary: protected nature area for monarch butterflies

Monarchs Across Georgia: a committee that works with teachers, students, families, communities, businesses, and others to study monarchs and restore butterfly habitat in Georgia. See eealliance.org/monarchs-across-ga.html

Monoculture: an area dominated by one species

Moult: shed its skin, or cuticle, (verb); or, the skin that has been shed (noun)

N

Native plant: a plant that grew in a region of North America before European settlers arrived in the 16th and 17th centuries

Naturalize: a naturalized plant is a non-native plant that does not need human help to reproduce and maintain itself over time in an area where it is not native. An example is a dandelion.

Nectar plant: a plant that produces sweet liquid eaten by adult butterflies, bees, hummingbirds, bats, and other animals

O

Ornamental plants: plants imported from other countries for the purpose of decoration. They are of little or no value to the food web and may become invasive.

Omnivore: an animal or person that eats food of both plant and animal origin

Organism: an individual plant, animal, or single-celled life form

Osmerterium: an orange forklike gland that emits a foul smell to ward off predators

Oviposit: lay eggs

P

Parasite: an organism that feeds off another, weakening or killing it

Parasitoid: an insect whose larvae live as parasites

Pheromones: a chemical released by an insect (or mammal) to affect the behaviour of creatures of the same species. Used to communicate, they may, for example, mark a territory or signal an alarm. They are best known for their ability to attract a mate.

Proboscis: the coiled, tubelike mouthpart of a butterfly that operates as a straw and wick

Proleg: short fleshy, unjointed leg attached to the abdomen of some insects

Propagation: the process of creating new plants

Pupa: the development stage between caterpillar and adult. In butterflies, the chrysalis.

Pupa dance: the gyrations of a newly developing chrysalis when it secures its cremaster and casts off the cuticle after the final moult

Pupal case: the covering in which a caterpillar transforms into a butterfly or moth

Pupate: moult for the last time, exposing the pupa within

Propagate: reproduce by natural processes

Puddling: sipping moisture from mud puddles, to take in salts and minerals from the soil

Purging: evacuating excess fluid

S

Spawn: deposit eggs

Spinneret: a silk-producing organ

Sapling: a young tree

X

Xerces Society: an international nonprofit organization that protects the natural world through the conservation of invertebrates and their habitats

U

Unesco (United Nations Educational, Scientific and Cultural Organization): a specialized agency of the United Nations aimed at promoting world peace and security through international cooperation in education, the sciences, and culture

Index

Acknowledgments

My inspiration comes from the tireless Drs. Chip Taylor, Doug Tallamy, and Richard Louv. Each of them created nature movements, and speak frequently to deliver their messages. My citizen scientist colleagues Don Davis, Edith Ellen Lee Smith, Brenda Dziedzic, Debbie Jackson, and Holli Hearn, continue to be generous with their time and skills. There are millions of others, whose efforts to conserve our planet motivate me to do my part.

I am grateful to the many people who contributed photographs to help make this book shine.

I wish to thank those who took the time to offer corrections and improvements to the manuscript: Chip Taylor, Todd Stout, Connie Hodson, Dan Bohlen, Phyllis Calvery, John Oysten, Doug Tallamy, Richard Louv, Lorraine Johnson, Don Davis, Dan Kraus, and Robert M. Pyle.

My sincere gratitude to publisher Sharon Fitzhenry for her vision. Together with talent and coaching from editor Charlene Dobmeier, designer Tanya Montini, and publisher Holly Doll, *5 Butterflies* came to life.

Praise for 5 Butterflies

'A beautiful book, from beginning to yet another beginning.'
–Dr. Richard Louv, author of best selling books, *Last Child in Woods* and *Our Wild Calling*.

'5 Butterflies will help you build a personal relationship
with the little things that run the world. Give it a try!'
—Professor Doug Tallamy, author of best selling books *Bringing Nature Home*, and *Nature's Best Hope*.

(Carol) '...is helping readers connect, or reconnect, with the natural world -
a path that if taken, will lead to exploration, wonder and enjoyment.'
—Dr. Orley R. 'Chip' Taylor, Founder of Monarch Watch, Professor Emeritus, The University of Kansas.

'an extraordinary introduction to nature' 'abundant and gorgeous photographs'
—Dr. David G. James, Associate Professor of Entomology, Washington State University - Prosser.

'If any book can inspire a love of nature in teenagers, this one will.
Carol has an infectious enthusiasm for the subject, and her passion
shines through in every sentence.'
—Dr. John Oyston, Past Vice-President, North American Native Plant Society.